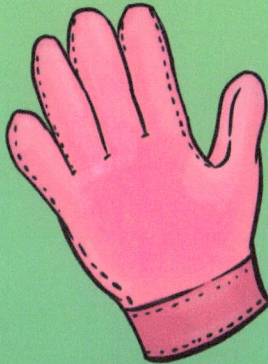

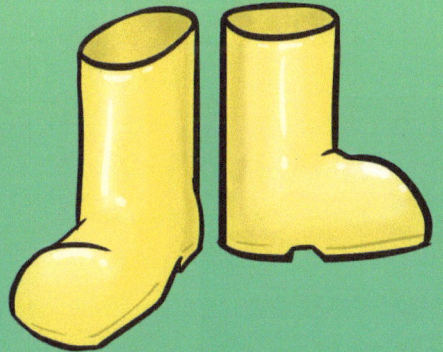

Quantity order requests can be emailed to:
publishing@rejilaberje.com
Reji Laberje Author Programs
Or mailed to:
Publishing Orders
234 W. Broadway Street
Waukesha, WI 53186

First Printing: 2007 by Reji Laberje
Laberje, Reji
Author: How Daisy Grew

Fenech, Liza
Illustrator: How Daisy Grew

ISBN: 0692676422
ISBN-13: 978-0692676424

Writing and Publishing
www.rejilaberje.com

How Daisy Grew

By Reji Laberje
Illustrations by Liza Fenech

For the girls of Troop 2492

Daisy's mom owned a greenhouse, beside their home outside of town. She loved to watch her mother work, so each day she would go down and - after cereal and getting dressed – she'd walk across the grounds, until she reached that special door that held behind its frame the sweetest scents in all the world; the brightest colors; and the tall, full flowers for which her mother held fame.

There was one in particular Daisy loved more than the rest. It had many colors and many petals and she knew that it was best for the place she dreamed of putting it; a place that only Daisy knew for it was her very own small, sweet special secret.

But, today, as Daisy came in, a customer went out and what was in her hand was enough to make Daisy shout: "Mom, how could you? That one's mine! I have watched it every day! I can't believe that you could let a stranger take it away!"

Daisy stomped and screamed and punched the air. She looked at the plot where the flower had been and, now, nothing was there. How could this happen, she thought, as her eyes began to tear? She frowned hard at her mother and said, "it just isn't fair."

"Now, Daisy," said her mother as she tried to calm her girl, "you know I wish that I could give you every flower in the world. But that one was for someone else. She paid me and it's hers. It's what your mother does here. You knew that. So, what's all this stir? You can't be out here like this. So, you have to go in, today. You think about a way to get your own flower that is fair and, maybe then, you can stay."

"But…" began Daisy. Then her mother waved
her away.

"I don't need to hear it, Daisy. Just promise me that you'll
think."

Daisy huffed and she jumped, but her mother didn't blink.
So, she sighed and said, "fine. I'll do my best. I promise,"
and she left to think.

So, on that next, first day – after cereal and getting dressed – Daisy went down to fix her tantrum's mess.

"Look who's back," said her mother with a smile but her eyes were stern.

Daisy didn't falter. "I'm sorry" she said. "But, I know how I can earn my time in here."

"I'm listening" said her mother and she really was.

"I thought I could grow a flower where my favorite one once was" she said timidly.

"Okay, Daisy, great" said her mother! "Now, that idea sounds fair, but it will take ten days, at least - before you'll notice in your plot there – a stem like a tiny, little, light green tree."

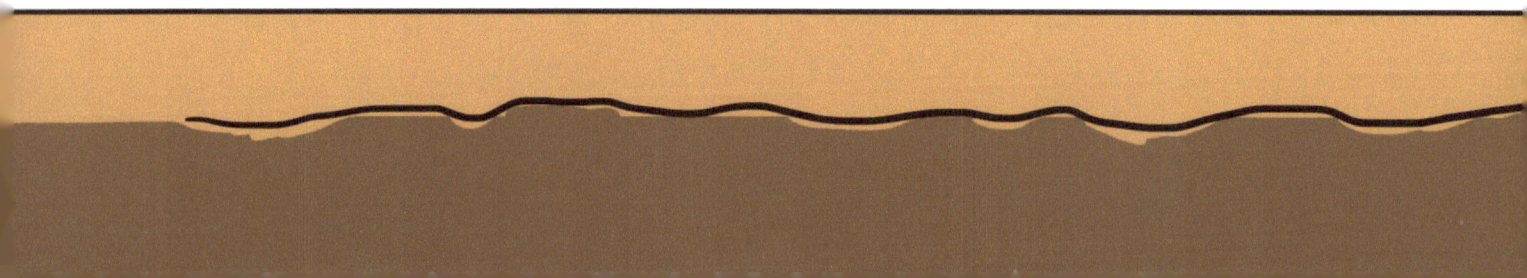

Her mother brought over a packet of seeds and Daisy raked her dirt. She dug a tiny little whole, put in some seeds and then covered them all.

She watered her seeds and she watched them all day until her mother said, "It's time to go, okay?"

On the second day – after cereal and getting dressed –
Daisy went down to see her
flower's success.

When no stem was born into that plot of earth, she knew
it was time to water once more.

"Come over here, Daisy," said her mother happily. "I'll show you how we do it when we water everything. Here, you take this bucket and stand down at the end of the whole entire row of plots. I'll water with the hose and then..."

As Daisy held the bucket on the ground beneath the last box, something neat happened that made her laugh in shock. There was a small drain through a hole beneath the plots and the extra water all poured out – there certainly was a lot. She followed her mother around each time that she pulled out the hose and Daisy would fill a bucket and use that water once more to care for other rows, and plots, and boxes, and free-standing trees.

When all of her mother's plants had been watered, Daisy asked her mother, "please, now that these are all done, can I water my new seeds?"

Her mother smiled and said, "of course. I just wanted to show you how to save the water, first."

On the third day – after cereal and getting dressed – Daisy went down to check on her tiny floral nest.

She watered in the way her mother taught her yesterday and, when she reached her own small flowerbed, she almost ran away.

"Nothing's happening!" she said to her mother. "Why bother, anyway? It's never gonna be a flower. Not now or any other day!"

"It's hard Daisy," began her mother, "to keep going when there's nothing to see. It takes courage to believe that your flower will soon be, but it will. Just believe in what you can do. And don't give up. It's too soon for that."

So, Daisy watered her plot and dug deep to find the courage to believe that her flower would be fine.

On the fourth day – after cereal and getting dressed –
Daisy returned with courage no matter what waited in
her best little greenhouse box.

There still wasn't a flower or stem to be seen, but when a
child came in and said in a voice that was mean, "why are
you bothering to water that thing? It's nothing but dirt! I
see nothing green!"

Daisy just smiled and said, "just dirt, now. But I believe it will be more somehow," and she went on watering and believing, too.

On the fifth day – Daisy had cereal and got dressed – but before she even got a chance to wet the dirt upon her seeds, she realized that her mother was very busy picking weeds.

She didn't need her mom to ask. She put on gloves and went to task. She pulled out weeds and swept up dirt. She smiled at her mother and then hugged her.

When all of the greenhouse work was done, Daisy took care of one last one...her tiny seeds beneath the dirt; she watered them and added food to the earth.

On the sixth day – instead of cereal and getting dressed – Daisy told her mother, "I don't feel the best."

She knew that she had promised, but she really wasn't sure that she could water all the plants when the room just seemed to swirl. Her head was hot and her throat felt fat and her tummy just said,"*GRR...*"

"Daisy," said her mother," you take a rest today. I'll help to water all the plants and you'll help another day."

So, Daisy stayed in bed and let her mother nurse. She nursed her head, and throat, and tummy, (and her flower, of course).

On the seventh day – after cereal and getting dressed –
Daisy decided that, though she still didn't feel her best,
she felt well enough to do what she had said.

So she went down to her mother in the greenhouse and
grabbed the bucket while her mother grabbed the hose.

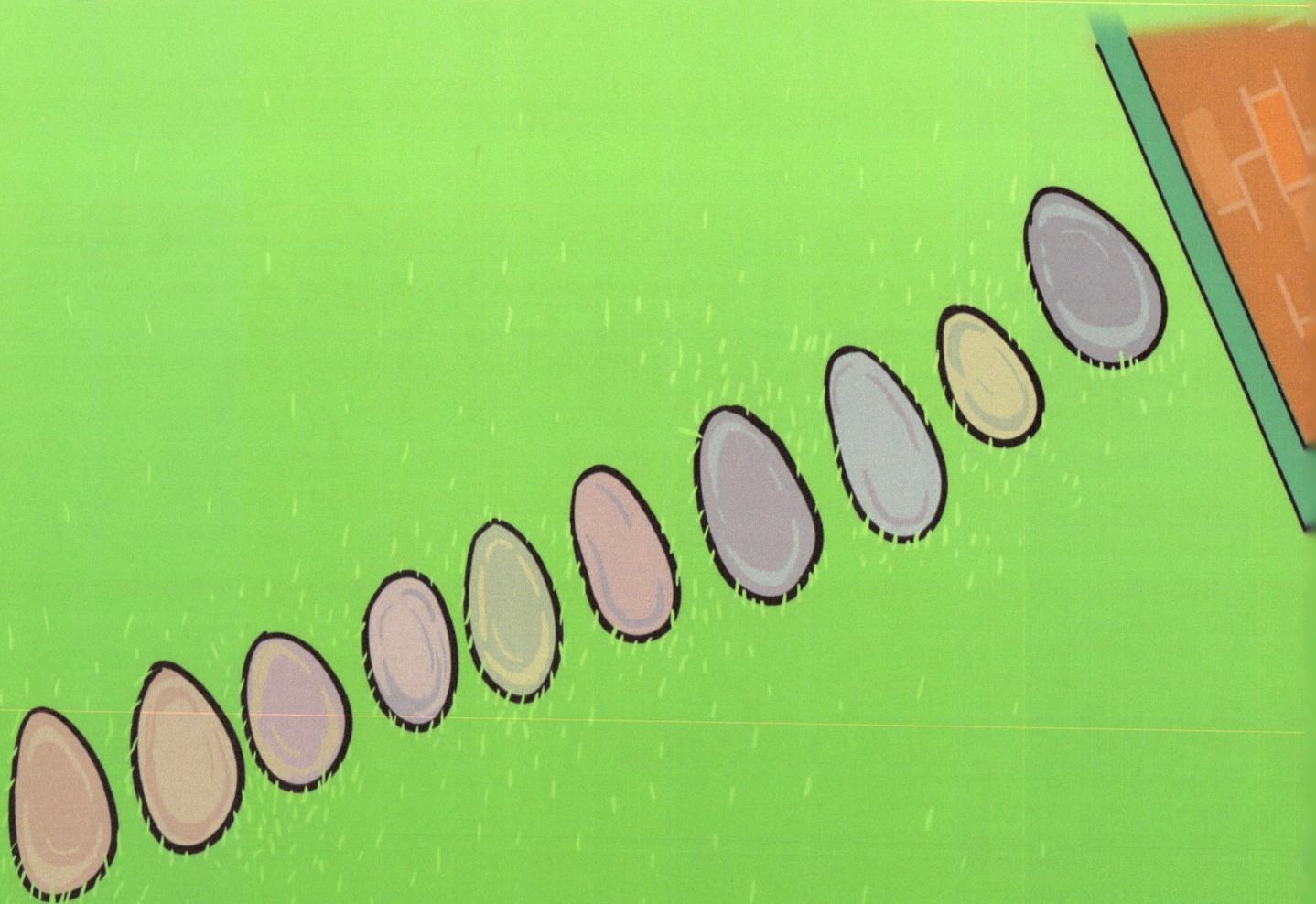

She didn't see the smallest little inkling of a sprig popping out from all that dirt, or a twig, or anything.

But she said that she would do her best and so, with courage strong, she cared for her plant as she had promised and hoped it would come along.

On the eighth day – after cereal and getting dressed – Daisy was a little tired, so she thought she wouldn't go down and she'd let her mom do all the watering, because she cared just for her own.

But her mother came looking for her around noon and asked "Daisy, darling, when will you be down? I count on my helper to water the plants. Without my young helper, I barely have a chance to get them all done. Won't you come out and lend me a hand?"

Daisy didn't want to, but she'd promised her mother that she'd do her best to grow her small flower. So, even though she'd have to help and water all of the plants, she knew it was better to do what was asked of her hard-working mother.

Daisy watered her seeds, still hidden in dirt, and she sighed and she yawned, but she finished her work.

On the ninth day – after cereal and getting dressed – Daisy sighed, for she was sure that this flower was just a test upon her patience and her hard work. Would she ever see the day that those young seeds would finally look like a tiny, little tree?

Instead of waiting for her mother to tell her what to do, she watered the plants and picked the weeds and swept up the dirt, too.

She finished finally at that spot that held her tiny seeds, beneath a tiny bit of dirt that Daisy hoped would heed that many-colored, many-petaled flower from her dreams.

She watered her seeds and she watched them all day until her mom said, "It's time to go, okay?"

On the tenth day, Daisy awoke smiling ear to ear. Her mother said that it would take ten days at least to see a stem like a tiny, little, light green tree.

So that day she went down and - after cereal and getting dressed – she walked across the grounds until she reached that special door that held behind its frame the sweetest scents in all the world; the brightest colors; and the tall, full flowers for which her mother held fame.

She ran right past her mother, to that tiny plot of dirt, to see if something special was waiting in that earth. When Daisy got to that last box, she smiled at her work. For something special had popped up that meant that it was worth the efforts she had put in and the time that she'd put forth.

There was a tiny, green stem there, but there was something else. The smallest bud Daisy had ever seen had opened up...nothing less. It was many-colored and many-petaled and she knew that it was best for the place she dreamed of putting it; a place that only Daisy knew for it was her very own small, sweet special secret.

"Mom, come here," she called! "And close your eyes! And open your hands 'cause I have a surprise!"

Without knowing what young Daisy would do, her mother did just what Daisy said to, and she held out her hands, and opened them up and then that Daisy yanked her flower right up. For the special place of which she dreamed was in the glow of her mother's gleam when she surprised her with the gift of the prettiest flower that she could give.

"It's your turn, Mom, to finally have what for, all your life, you only gave."

With eyes full of tears, and a heart simply full, Daisy's mom smiled down at her little girl.

"Daisy, you grew a flower! You could...I always knew! But I guess I never realized how much that flower would grow you."

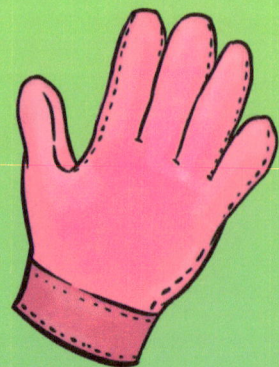

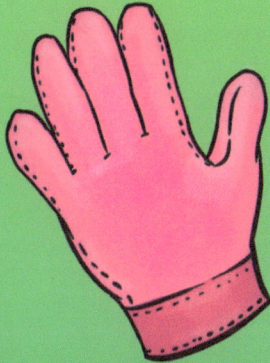

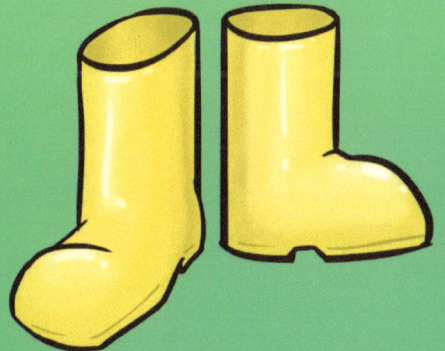

www.ingramcontent.com/pod-product-compliance
Lightning Source LLC
Chambersburg PA
CBHW041547040426
42447CB00002B/81